A TOTAL LIFE

Four Timeless Principles

Live A Life Without Tradeoffs

Louis C. Baker

The Inspire Media Group

Publishing House is the exclusive license holder of the

Federally registered trademark A TOTAL LIFE

ISBN: 1-4392-4919-9

ISBN-13: 9781439249192

Visit www.booksurge.com to order additional copies.

All contents and rights owned in entirety by

Inspire Media Group

Established January 1, 2003 in Newport Beach, CA

Address:

260 Newport Center Dr.

Newport Beach, CA 92660

Ph: 949.929.4792

SPECIAL THANKS

I WANT TO THANK ALL MY MENTORS
INCLUDING BUT NOT LIMITED TO:

ERIC CARTER
JEVON PERRA
JENNIFER JEFFRIES
ADAM AYERS
ADAM NILI
LAUREN HOLLEY
AARON JAMES
JESSE PIKE
MICHAEL GRANIERI
RON JENSEN
ED BROWER
DOUG SALISBURY
DORAN ANDRE

SPECIAL THANKS TO ENNIO SOLUCCI
FOR ALL HIS SUPPORT

AND GOD

TABLE OF CONTENTS

ABOUT THE AUTHOR

Louis is a real estate investor with a background in financial planning. Having worked with Cruttenden Roth, Mercer Global Advisors, and Merrill Lynch, Louis focused primarily on small- to mid-level investment banking, stock options, and restricted stock planning. While at Merrill Lynch, Louis worked as an advocate for fifteen *elite net worth*[1] families.

Louis is the founder of Charles Property Group, a real estate, investment, and property management company. He is also the founder of several other companies including: The Anodos Group, Traker Development, and Inspire Media Group. After over fifteen years in financial services, and entrepreneurial adventures Louis is most excited about pursuing and helping others pursue *A Total Life*.

Louis is the father of two, just finished a 12 song piano cd, and is currently working on an inspiration folk cd with guitar and vocals. He hopes this writing is only the beginning of a life of putting ideas to paper. His vision is to inspire, motivate and encourage individuals to take positive action. Please visit him at any of the below:

Trakerdevelopment.com
Charlesfinancialgroup.com
Charlespropertygroup.com
Charlesproperty.net
Inspiremediagroup.com
Facebook: Louis Baker, Orange County
louisbakerthemusic.blogspot.com

---

1   See glossary

FOREWORD

In thinking about life and what it is all about, I have come to believe that all men and women should discover what it is that they can leave behind for the next generation or the next adventurer. Some leave behind buildings, some appear in movies, and others create music, poetry, or other timeless gifts. After much evaluation and thought, I have decided to leave an idea behind in the form of a book, and that idea is that of *A Total Life*. What I offer is myself and what I have are my thoughts on how I see life and the world. These observations have come through constant examination, continual reading, life experiences, and a general care for others. I believe for some there is freedom in this work because the ideas when understood help people rediscover their passions and live more exciting happy lives.

As a young man I was always desperately searching for mentors. I was looking for people I could model my life after, and in my search I found and walked with many great men and women. After years of watching these individuals and growing with them, I started to respect each mentor and role model for their specific respective strengths. For example, one individual was amazing with her financial affairs, another had a great marriage, another was healthy and yet another really had his spiritual life together. What was so interesting was none of my early mentors had it all. It seems each them was lacking either wealth, health, spirituality or relationship success.

At some point I started to think about finding someone who had it all. Who can I model my life after who isn't making any trade-offs? Which of these men or women are healthy, happy, wealthy, fun, spiritual, have great relationships, and more? After years of searching I discovered men and women who had it all, who were living A Total

Life. This book is about Four Timeless Principles they all used to achieve total, complete, multifaceted lives.

My legacy is my thoughts that have been developed through friendships, business, pain, sadness, success, betrayal, and a constant yearning for truth. In this writing are my hopes for my children, my dreams for my friends, and my love for humanity and all of us who have a deep longing for more.

Another Note:

I have formatted this book like a journal in that there are many blank pages in the book for you to write on and record your thoughts or ideas. You may want to skip around, read a chapter multiple times, or just keep this book as a journal for your thoughts. I have found that books can become secret depositories for ideas and thoughts. I hope this book will serve you in this way as well.

INTRODUCTION

A Total Life is an idea that comes from analyzing those who have a complete, multifaceted, and inclusive life and not simply a high level of success in one area. Let us look at this concept of *A Total Life* a little deeper. Webster defines *total* as, "involving all aspects, elements, participants, resources, etc.; unqualified; all-out; total war." Think about the concept of total war. Being at total war would mean you and all your troops would be fighting with all your energy, passion, heart, and everything—leaving nothing on the table. Part of *A Total Life* is about the way you do things (i.e., the way you live) and has nothing to do with what you do. Now let us look at *life*. Webster defines *life* as, "the course of existence or sum of experiences and actions that constitute a person's existence." Furthermore, most of life can be broken down into four major categories including relationships, health, wealth, and spirituality. Based on these definitions of *total* and *life*, I developed this concept of *A Total Life*:

> *Living a life with a high level of peace and competency*
> *in one's relationships, health, wealth, and spirituality, and*
> *holding nothing back*
> *in any moment*
> *over one's lifetime.*

Let us look at each of the elements of *A Total Life* separately so that each aspect is clear as to what to strive for or attempt to acquire.

Relationships: This category is comprised of how we relate to others. Our friends, family, co-workers, pastor, priest, rabbi, girlfriend, boyfriend, spouse, children, community relationships, neighbors, and more all fall under the relationship category.

Health: This category refers to ones physiology, their physical well being. Topics such as exercise, stretching, diet, athletics, monitoring, maintenance, appearance, and the like all fall under the health component.

Wealth: Under this category, we find all the concepts around wealth, such as money, investing, borrowing, lending, insurance, legacy planning, estate planning, and taxes. At the core, the wealth category encompasses things like the acquisition of large sums of money and the knowledge to maintain and continually grow and use the funds acquired.

Spirituality: This category is a bit misleading because more is included here than one might expect. Wisdom, hope, intelligence, faith, character, values, principles, giving, serving, loving, and all things that are not specifically in the other three categories are considered spirituality.

Given the explanation of the above categories, let us look at the definition of *A Total Life* one more time.

> *Living a life with a high level of peace and competency*
> *in one's relationships, health, wealth and spirituality*
> *holding nothing back*
> *in any moment*
> *over one's lifetime.*

A Total Life is the result of a life of research and intense examination with many diverse people from many varied backgrounds. From my experiences and research, four key timeless principles rose to the surface as the critical elements to creating *A Total Life*. These principles are *Design Your Life*, *Vision vs. Vice*, *Integration*, and *Aware-ness*. This book is primarily about understanding these key timeless principles and becoming aware of how to implement them on your journey toward *A Total Life*. Why go after *A Total Life*? Why not settle for a good life? These questions will be answered as you begin to explore the first principle, *Design Your Life*. You will find that your choices and decisions create the life you live, and the *Design* you follow will create the destination you arrive at.

A Total Life is in contrast to a *balanced* life in that a balanced life asks one to give up in one area in order to get back to balance in another. Balance is the idea of stopping one thing, like working, and starting another, like going to the gym, in order to get balanced. The concepts in *A Total Life* ask the individual not to stop one thing to attain another, but rather to find a better way to win at both without drawing back in one area.[2]

Unlike many personal growth books and other achievement-oriented literature, this book urges its readers to win in all areas of life and not just in one area such as finances, health, spirituality, or relationships. It challenges the commonly held notion that to win in one sphere of life necessitates making a *trade-off*, a sacrifice, of another aspect of life, such as trading off time with your family or neglecting your health in pursuit of money. Having *A Total Life* is not about making a *trade-off*. This book is about *designing* your life to have it all. Cuba Gooding Jr. said it in the movie *Jerry McGuire*, "Jerry, I want it all; I want the quan." The *quan* was a word Cuba's character used to describe what the elite athletes in the NFL had. The *quan* represented the life and attitude of those athletes who had all the fame, prestige, endorsements, respect, and appreciation year after year

---

2   Overall balance is a good concept as long as you are shooting for balance at a high level in all areas

after year. Athletes like Peyton Manning of the Indianapolis Colts or Brett Favre of the Green Bay Packers define the quan. We have all seen great athletes throw their careers away after getting caught up in drugs, drunk driving, and other scandals that leave them stripped of their hard earned athletic success. With regard to *A Total Life*, the way you go about achieving success and the way you behave and act in the role are equally as important as the individual achievements themselves.

Unlike many books that simply outline quick-fix strategies to make, invest, keep, and protect wealth, this book delivers a more *Integrated* approach, which enables the reader to a achieve success without just making more money. To pursue *A Total Life* might be one of the most challenging and difficult endeavors you have ever embarked upon because the goal is not specific and the path is not simple. Many ingredients go into the recipe for a life worth savoring. These ingredients, however, are different for everyone, but by implementing the four principles in this book, *Design Your Life, Vision vs. Vice, Integration, and Awareness*, you can truly begin the process of personal exploration, which is the foundation for living and discovering *A Total Life*.

Most self help books deal with either "bottom-line" matters, which include things such as investments, retirement, tax-saving strategies, real estate optimization, health insurance, life insurance, and inheritance issues, or with "top-line" matters, which include purpose, vision, legacy, values, health, religion, and so on. What these kinds of books fail to recognize, however, is the way in which these bottom-line and top-line issues affect and influence each other in dramatic and inevitable ways.

This book's intent is to lay out key principles that, when understood and lived fully, help create *A Total Life*. It deals with the numerous elements that comprise both bottom-line and top-line issues in such a way as to assure that you will not have worked hard to earn a living and missed out on true living in the process.

You will feel good as you read this book and uncover the four simple principles: *Design your Life, Vision vs. Vice, Integration*, and *Awareness,* because this book will help you gain clarity as to what you want and how to get it.[3] In addition, you will feel encouraged to *Design* an amazing future for your life, one that will inspire you and motivate you to take charge and take action. Your new *Life Design* and *Vision* will create possibilities and energy that will fuel your life at a level that surprises even you! A phrase that could be used to describe what you are about to engage in is *life audit* or *possibility exploration*. You are going to explore, challenge, and question what you now hold as true. You are going to examine, uncover, and open yourself up to all the possibilities of your life, and what is so great is that you will do it all on your own terms.

The principles outlined in this book will prove essential to your ability to *Design* the life you know is possible and have longed to enjoy because they are developed in a logical, linear way to help you engage one step at a time, starting with your *Design*. No untried concepts are offered here, only life examples and sound practical advice that make clear what works, what does not work, what you should avoid, and what is indispensable. You will probably notice as you read this book that the life you long for is attainable and closer than you thought possible. You will feel inspired when it becomes clear that you may be only a few decisions away from completely embracing all that is possible for yourself. *Up until now*, you may have been held back by limiting beliefs, negativity, pessimistic friends, fear, greed, or a lack of purpose, *but now* you can create the life you long for.

Up Until Now/But Now Concept

---

3   This is because there are exercises throughout the book

Up until now and *but now* can be some of the most powerful words someone can use when he or she decides to pursue *A Total Life*. For example: *up until now* I worked for someone else, *but now* I have a plan to work for myself; *up until now* I have had a boring marriage, *but now* my marriage is becoming exciting and passionate; *up until now* I was overweight, *but now* I feel healthy and am getting in great shape.

After reading this, you might find yourself wanting to use the blank pages to write down some *up until now/but now* statements for yourself, and I encourage you to do so. This book is intended to give you the opportunity to write down your thoughts and ideas; it can be used as a journal or scrapbook. Have fun and mark this book up as much as possible.

It is my hope that as you read this book and engage in the various exercises, you will begin to find a new hope, a new vision, and a belief that you can do anything you put your mind and heart to. I hope you will feel refreshed and a developed sense of freedom, as if you are getting a second chance to live a different life. The life you desire is both possible and attainable. I invite you to read on.

HOW THE BOOK CAN WORK FOR YOU

When applied, the principles and concepts in this book are life transforming. To understand how to apply the principles I must introduce you to two terms I use in my friendships. One term is "walking" with. If I am walking with a friend, we are spending time together under a shared concept that we both believe in. I would use the term like this, "Tom and I are *walking* together under the concepts of inspiring, motivating and encouraging others to make great choices. This means we are spending a lot of time together and are committed to a friendship in light of the above concepts. The other term I use is "doing life" with. If I am *doing life* with a friend, that friend is totally current and completely included in everything I do. For example, I might say, "Tom and I are *doing life* together, so I suspect he will be at all the meetings next week." Doing life with someone has nothing to do with a shared idea; it is more of a commitment to be totally current and completely included in someone's life.

Having said that, the best way to engage with this book is by memorizing the principles and then *doing life* with them by consistently applying them to every life-scenario you experience or envision. Keep current with them and always keep them with you. When you have memorized the concepts, you will be amazed at how simply and easily they will help you. These concepts can be conceived of as "Umbrella Principles" that you can use for shelter and guidance throughout your life journey. As you apply them, you will find yourself walking in *Total Life s*uccess, actually living *A Total Life*:—feeling great, open to possibilities, free of fear, and excited about the future.

The four principles are:

1. DESIGN YOUR LIFE	3. INTEGRATION
2. VISION VS. VICE	4. AWARENESS

WHAT WE TRULY EARNESTLY ASPIRE TO BE, THAT, IN
SOME SENSE WE ARE.
ANNA JOHNSTON

WHEN YOU DETERMINE WHAT YOU WANT YOU HAVE
MADE THE MOST IMPORTANT DECISION IN YOUR LIFE.
DOUGLAS LURTON

notes

DESIGN YOUR LIFE

Key concept: It begins in the mind.
Your mind creates thoughts; those thoughts become ideas;
ideas become beliefs; beliefs become actions; actions become
character; and character becomes legacy.

HOW IT WORKS

The concept of *Designing* your life is not a concept to make you unhappy or discontent with your current life. *A Total Life* is not some place at which you will arrive; rather it is more of an ideal, a grand concept worthy of pursuit. To have joy, intimacy, connectedness, fun, money, health, spiritual wholeness, legacy, and more is not easy, and the goal is not to tirelessly strive to get them. The real idea is to pursue them, to enjoy the process, and to walk with others in the pursuit. The goal is to humbly learn and grow with each other in light of this grand ideal—*A Total Life*.

A Total Life is one in which you are not making *trade-offs* and settling for the predictable. *A Total Life* is one in which you are not making choices out of fear or lack of awareness. The principle of *Design Your Life* may seem arrogant in that I am suggesting that much of the positive life results are in the hands of the individuals rather than global, social, and other circumstances. However, I am just asking us all to control the parts we can and not the parts we cannot.

Obviously, if a hurricane hit your town, you did not *Design* it to happen, or if you are robbed or accidentally hurt, you did not plan it or *Design* it. I do not believe you *Design* every part of your world; however, you can *Design* the best responses to unfortunate situations. *Designing* responses that help you quickly move out of the **Victim Role**[4] and into the ***Design* role** can help you to not live as a victim of circumstances and free you to

4   see glossary

notes

continue to pursue your *Design*. For example, pretend you were robbed at gunpoint and lost your wallet and some very important sentimental items. You could allow that incident to define your life negatively for years to come or you could simply think, "That happened, but now I am back to my goals, my vision, my future." You also could think, "*Up until now*, when negative, difficult things happened to me, I used to dwell on them, feel sorry for myself, tell everyone I knew, and feel horrible, *but now* I simply find what I can learn from the situation and then re-engage with the *Total Life* I am pursuing."

The reason obtaining *A Total Life* begins with *Design* is that without ownership of our life and our outcomes, we may find it difficult to honor the moments we have. It is like leasing a car. When you know you are not the owner, you tend to treat the car more poorly and oftentimes recklessly. In addition, because you are not the owner, you take less responsibility if something goes wrong with the car. Many of us are living life as if we do not own it, like we are just borrowing our life, and when something goes wrong it is not really our fault. *Design* creates a feeling of ownership and ownership creates a spirit of stewardship and honor. When we honor and steward our lives toward a worthy ideal, we can achieve the impossible and leave the predictable to the renters. So when you start the *Design* process, own up to a *Design* that is worthy of the life that is yours. Do not *trade off* intimacy, joy, and love for money, and do not *trade off* health and money for spiritual connectedness. Go for *A Total Life*. We are not going to live forever, so *Designing* our life helps us take ownership of it and prevents us from

notes

having a life of regrets. Make concrete choices, decisive decisions, set goals, use time lines, and have fun with your *Design*. Once you have been free to *Design* unfettered from worries, fears, and your history, we will tackle the biggest roadblocks getting in the way of your plan being implemented—V*ices*.

....

notes

The path to *Total Life* success begins with examining your current life. The most resourceful platform to examine your life is one that recognizes that your current state of life has been arrived at because of how you have *designed* it to be. What do I mean by *Design*? Let me give you an example of how much design plays into what one receives or gets out of life.

If you worked at the cash register at McDonalds for twenty years and worked as hard as you could, you probably would not have tens of millions of dollars—hard work does not equal large profits or great financial success. The *Design* of a cash register job at McDonalds is such that great financial wealth is not available no matter how hard you work. If you have a small shot glass and you want to fill it with an ocean of possibilities, it would be impossible because the glass can only hold a small amount of water. This analogy explains why so many of us who have energy, drive, and charisma fail in our attempts to accomplish our hopes and dreams—our *Design* is like a small shot glass. What is needed is a better, larger *Design*—a swimming pool or a lake so that we do not outperform our *Design*. If you worked really hard selling airplanes or large commercial buildings, you could generate millions and millions of dollars with the same effort as working at McDonalds. The *Design* is more important than the effort. We all need to work hard, that is a given, but it is even more vital that we have solid *Designs* for our relationships, our health, our finances, and our spiritual and community building endeavors.

I have a friend who is almost sixty years old who looks like he is less than forty. His skin is perfect, his body is in great shape, and he has an amazing spirit about him. How is this possible, you may

. . . .

notes

ask? It is simple. He is following the *Design* of his mentor, who is now eighty and looks like he is fifty. His mentors design included things like eating raw foods, stretching, creative breathing techniques, enzyme supplementation, and much more. What is so amazing is how good one can feel when the appropriate *Design* is in place.

I once heard someone say that we are getting either healthier or sicker. Do you have a plan to feel better or a plan just to get by? Although it may appear that you just happen to find yourself in the life that you are currently leading, from *A Total Life* perspective, you have *Designed* your life to be the way it is in every aspect—relational, physical, financial, emotional, and spiritual.

What do I mean by *Design*? I mean what you have set yourself to, what you have held in your mind, and what you have determined. You may be saying, "No way!" You may even argue that you have not proactively taken any steps to make your life the way it is and instead have just let things unfold until this time. While this may be unarguably true, the assertion remains. Your life is the way it is currently not merely because of random events, but because of how you have *Designed* it to be. This *Designing* begins in your thoughts and manifests in your life through the choices you have made as a result of those thoughts. It is not the way it is (your life) due to the circumstances you have found yourself in or due to the hand that has been dealt to you.

The proof for this assertion is simple—if life were simply determined by mere circumstances then everyone with similar circumstances would have the same life. Clearly, this is not the case. It is not even true for people raised in the same family, by the same parents, who have similar intellectual gifts, and who have been given the same

notes

opportunities. It is not true for people with similar disabilities and abilities. Some prosper and excel while others languish. Obviously, something distinguishes one person's results from another's. That something is the *Design* that each person set out to accomplish, and regardless of whether it was a conscious or subconscious *Design*, the plan will play out.

One man, from whom I learned much about *Total Life* success, told me his childhood story. He grew up in the poorest of poor farming families in Idaho. He lived in a shack with garbage stacked in his front yard. The entire town knew that his home was in the slums. Although his father was a competent farmer, his financial skills were terrible and creditors and loan sharks constantly stopped by. When he came of age, his father gave him a shot at creating his own wealth, giving him a plot of land of his own to work. After tirelessly working the farm and putting his entire lifeblood into the plot of land, a hailstorm came through and destroyed the crops and his hopes of harvest.

How many of you have experienced something similar? You diligently work your fingers to the bone, doing all you know how, and something beyond your control comes along and dashes your expectations. That something could be the loss of a job, friend, or family member; a sudden sickness or injury; a business deal gone bad; or a betrayal—anything that derails you from what you were so excited about attaining.

Without any money and worrying about survival, this man faced a tough choice—stay with what he knew and hope that fate would treat him more kindly in the future or take a leap into the unknown.

notes

Determined to find a way to break the legacy passed down to him, he chose to leave home and chance it in the world rather than starve where he was. His dad, learning that his sixteen-year-old son was going to leave the farm, his family, and the state to head west, gave him two hundred dollars and asked him not to spend it if he did not have to.

This man went on to become one of the most successful eye surgeons in the world, pioneering ground breaking techniques in his field, with inventions and patents making him tens of millions of dollars. And what is so interesting to note is that in his pride and determination, he accomplished what he did without ever spending one dollar of his dad's money. When I asked him how he accomplished so much, he simply said, "I did not want the life my parents had."

Some of you may be saying, "Well that's great, but I have all the money I need. I just can't seem to meet someone with whom to share it." The *Design* flaw at play with this thinking goes something like this: "I need to work hard, put my head down, and make something of myself so later I can enjoy the fun, passionate, exciting life with my future partner." The problem is, while you are learning all about how to generate income and be valuable in the world, your "be great in relationship skills" are not being cultivated. Therefore, when it is time to jump in the dating relationship game you may not understand affirmation, appreciation, affection, listening, requests, relational conflict resolution, and all the other key components needed to make a relationship full, lasting, and awesome. Again, your *Design* dictates what you will get in life, so the importance of critically assessing your current *Design* cannot be overemphasized. Your circumstances really

notes

....

do not matter. Ask yourself if you want the life your circumstances dictate or do you want the life you *Design?* What do you want? What do you want?

It is okay if you are not yet totally convinced that your life is a result of how you have *Designed* it. Right now, all that is needed from you is to consider this assertion as a possibility, to move into it, and then see what unfolds for you. This is the time to begin to think differently. When you do not try to think differently, the only possibilities you will open up are variations of the ones you have already opened—leading to a future that looks similar to what you have always experienced in the past. In order to think differently, you must challenge what you believe to be true and even your concept of reality.

POSSIBILITY EXPLORATION

What kind of life do you want? What are the possibilities? *Total Life* success begins with "possibility exploration." What is a possibility? Exactly what it sounds like—something you can imagine. It is certainly not a limited view of what you or others can achieve in a given amount of time, space, or over a lifetime. It is an expansive, open, free, uninhibited discovery of what one can be, do, or have. A possibility is freedom! Freedom to dream and conceive, unfettered by the past and independent from present limitations. A possibility is something that exists because you envision it. It is something that is "invented" in the mind. Every great achievement in history and every great accomplishment of humankind began from a *Vision Designed* in the mind.

....

notes

All the great accomplishments of history have been achieved by men and women who developed a *Vision*, from Columbus, who envisioned discovering a new world; to the Pilgrims, who pictured a society where they could practice their religion freely; to our founding fathers, who saw a nation run by a government "of the people, by the people, for the people." All these people saw something in their mind's eye that enabled them to change the course of their destiny and the destinies of countless others.

On one point, however, I need to be very clear; a *Vision* without congruent actions that will foster its coming to reality is more like a daydream. Many great leaders and innovators had difficulty getting their projects to completion. For most there was a period of failure and discouragement as well as time before their conception became a reality. Although it is crucial to have a vision and an idea of what you want in your mind, the follow up is also important as well. Below is an example of how a great idea and the execution of that idea can and should work together.

THE CHAIR

Imagine how the chair was invented. Probably a man or woman thought, as he or she sat on a log or a rock, "It would sure be nice to have my feet resting comfortably on the ground while my legs were relaxed. And what would make it even better is to have something to lean my back against." That person probably pictured what it would take to have this idea come to be, and then set out to create what he or

notes

she envisioned. In order for his or her feet to rest on the ground, the seat had to be elevated. The seat also had to be stabilized so that this person would not fall over as he or she put full weight on it. The place to rest his or her back also had to be able to sustain the weight of a person leaning on it. In a very real way, it was the *Vision* that dictated what was needed. Sure, the actual process of building the chair made clearer what worked and what did not, but in essence, the chair was created in the mind.

Real estate developers really understand the concept of *Design* because they add value to vacant land with their ideas. They purchase vacant land and create an idea, a community, a culture, a *Vision*. They then work tirelessly to get the *Vision*, the plan, approved by the city or county administrators. They then decide if they are going to develop any part of the plan. Oftentimes, after the plan is developed in the mind and on paper, it is sold to someone else who completes the project. What is so amazing is how much the *Design*, the "idea," can be worth. Sometimes hundreds of millions of dollars are generated just by *Designing* a concept for a piece of land. I have been fortunate enough to interact with individuals who make millions of dollars a month just by adding vision and creativity to real estate. What is so great is after they are done with the concept, most cities and counties will give developers ten years to build the city, housing project, amusement park, or whatever the approved plans necessitates. The idea lasts for ten years and sometimes more.

Real estate developers add value through *Vision*. Are you doing this in your life? Are you making yourself more valuable by creating a *Design* for your life that makes it more valuable? Most of us at one

....

notes

time have been in the dating scene. Is it not true that a person with a clear *Vision* for their life is more attractive than someone just floundering through life? YES! We can add immense value to who we are through *Design*, even if we do not implement our *Vision* for years and years. Just how vacant land with a clear drawn out plan is worth more than blank land, your life is worth more with a plan.

The better, more creative, dynamic, and inspiring the plan, the more valuable it is. If you are like most people, when you consider possibilities you use the past as a reference point to inform you about what is possible for you and what is not. Do not do that! Think about what you want and consistently go after it regardless of the past. Otherwise without knowing it, you may automatically omit possibilities because your past experiences dictate what you think is possible and impossible for you. In fact, your idea of really going for it is probably a variation of the past—more, better, or different, but still tied to the past. For example, it's time to get rid of the old coat, the one that makes you feel really comfortable but doesn't match up to the life you want to live. The old coat may represent a location, group of friends, habit, relationship or something that keeps you in place, is familiar, but really isn't helping you get the results you want. What is so amazing is how good you will feel when you start dreaming, let go of how things used to be, and grasp and focus on how things can and will be. It's time for a new coat.

The cynic would say that it is not good to encourage unattainable dreams and possibilities, or to fuel the unrealistic and fan the fantastic. As you read the next section, you will see why I disagree with the cynics. Our future experiences, environments, successes, and

notes

possibilities are created in our minds. Everything new that has been created began in someone's mind. Each one of the dreamers faced the naysayer. Look at these examples:

"Flight by machines heavier than air is unpractical and insignificant, if not utterly impossible." *Simon Newcomb, Astronomer, 1902*

"It is an idle dream to imagine that...automobiles will take the place of railways in the long distance movement of passengers." *American Road Congress, 1913*

"Who wants to hear actors talk?" *Harry Warner, Warner Brothers Pictures, 1927*

"I think there is a world market for about five computers." *Thomas J. Watson, Chairman of IBM, 1943*

Possibility thinkers have crosshairs on their chest aimed at them by people who do not want their world disturbed. As Albert Einstein noted, "Great spirits have always encountered violent oppression from mediocre minds!" The cynics are going to crucify your dreaming and idealism. Their aim is to keep you from flying so they can stay comfortable. They are like the crabs in the open-air markets in Mexico that never escape, even though they are great climbers and the baskets that contain them have no lids. They do not escape because when one crab tries to climb out of the basket, the other crabs pull him back in. This is just like life; your closest friends will try to keep you with

notes

them, for good or bad. The rule of thumb states that you will be at the same level of wealth, intelligence, and success as your top five friends. Make sure your best friends are where you want to be. It's the same with sports. For example, in tennis, you always want to play with a hitting partner that's at your level or better than you are so that your game is always improving. What is important is that you allow yourself to be surrounded by people who can pull you out of the basket. If you have great friends in both spheres you can always go and visit the old friends because your new ones will always pull you out. Do not get stuck with people who keep you limited and trapped and drain your energy.[5]

You will have the same problem with the naysayer. If they are not with you, they are in your way. You cannot judge them or even criticize them, but you can go after your *Vision* regardless of what they say. So, DO NOT BE AFRAID; instead, dare to dream. Start writing your possibilities, what you want out of life, and do not stop until you cannot say anything more. Memorize them, dream about them, and DO NOT BE AFRAID. What is the opposite of possibility? FEAR. What is the opposite of *Vision?* FEAR. Fear kills *Vision*, passion, fun, and purpose—the main things life has to offer. Fear is what many lives are made of—fear of not being enough, not being worthy, not meeting parental expectations, etc. If you are living out of fear, you have thrown in the white towel, but are still in the ring getting pummeled by life. It is a lose-lose situation.

---

5   I'm not saying get rid of your old trusted friends just make sure all your friends are not struggling to only survive day to day. Spend time with dreamers, creators, and innovators as well

....

notes

So write all you dreams hopes and possibilities down and then start failing or succeeding now. Yes, you may fail before you succeed. *It is better to fail at the impossible than to succeed at the predictable.* The pathway to *Total Life* success requires one to continually reframe his or her notion of failure as a learning experience. Give yourself freedom and permission to do what it takes to succeed, including learning from your mistakes and being okay when you make them. Consider the examples that follow.

Tom Watson Sr. was the guiding hand in the success of IBM for forty years. He knew the risks associated with business and the value of learning from mistakes. One year, a young executive was given responsibility for a project that cost over ten million dollars. As it turned out, the idea failed, and when the young man was called into the office, he quickly offered his resignation. "You can't be serious," said Watson. "We've just spent ten million dollars educating you!"

When Thomas Edison was trying to invent the electric light, he made thousands of mistakes before he had any success. Imagine how he had to reframe his failures after thousands of unsuccessful efforts to find the right filament. Edison failed ten thousand times before the invention of the light bulb.

Gail Borden made countless business blunders before achieving success with condensed milk and Milton Hershey failed more than once in the candy making business before finding success with the Hershey bar. If you are not failing, you are not dreaming, and if you are not dreaming, you are probably just surviving in life.

What is failure anyway? Too often, it is something we have decided, most likely as little children, which defines us. But consider

notes

that in basketball, failing 50 percent of the time is regarded as great, and in baseball, the best hitters fail 70 percent of the time! Many millionaires experienced bankruptcy before they made it. How many failed flights did the Wright brothers suffer?

The opposite of fear is not some crazy, needless, out of control risk-taking that leads to nowhere and gets nothing accomplished. It is daring to accomplish things that may seem impossible given your upbringing, your current resources, and your beliefs. However, fear, primarily fear of failure, keeps people from daring to dream of great things, and instead prompts settling for some attainable goal that makes life tolerable. Most people find a level of despair they can tolerate and call it happiness.

WORST CASE SCENARIO PLAN

If you are still struggling with fear, try completing some type of *worst-case scenario plan*[6].

It is simple to do. Just start with this question: If I lost everything and was naked on the street what would I do? Better yet, if you died last week, but had a chance to come back and live another thirty years, how would you live your life?

Many of the greatest accomplishments of all time have come from fearless people with great *Vision*. Fearlessness comes from facing the worst case scenario unflinchingly, seeing it as a possibility, and

---

6   See glossary

notes

determining that you would survive, and begin again, should the worst case scenario unfold.

There is real power accessed by people who have nothing to lose. They throw themselves into their *Vision* with abandon. This works for accomplishing great good and great evil. It was said that Lenin, speaking of the total commitment required to change the world for the cause of communism said, *"I do not care if the masses believe. Give me but twenty men who regard themselves as…'dead men on furlough' and I will change the world."* Is not our cause worthy of our very lives?

A Total Life begins by inventing, in your mind, what your life could look like. How much money will you have? What kind of relationships? What is the state of your health? What difference will you make in the world? What legacy will you leave? Take some time right now and do a "possibility exploration."

One of my clients wrote this as his possibility exploration:

> *It is possible that I could change my world by changing what I think. It is possible for me to be successful in every sphere of my life, to be a great husband, father, businessman, and be healthy, spiritually connected, giving, thankful, trustworthy, happy, forgiving, passionate, generous, and bold. I can achieve all these things without losing my relationships, health, or connection with God. I can be a world famous speaker and motivator, and experience inspiration at a level that amazes me daily. I can have*

notes

a beautiful ocean front home and businesses worth tens of millions. I can help others achieve the same success and live each day as if it were my last.

HAVE DO AND BE

Have you finished your exploration yet? If not, write it out now. Please do not worry about how you will achieve these possibilities, just write them down on the blank page. Doing so will make them more concrete. If you are still having trouble writing out your possibilities, start by writing out fifteen things you **want to have**, fifteen things **you want to do**, and fifteen ways **you want to be** in the next five, ten, fifteen, and twenty years.[7] Your possibility exploration does not have to seem reasonable to you. It does not have to appear to be within reach; in fact, if it is, you are merely doing a *probability* exploration. So, go ahead—imagine away…fear not…reach for the life you long for.

WHY I CAN'T/HOW I WILL EXERCISE

Now that you have imagined and *Designed* your *Total Life*, all of the old reasons for why "it can't happen" and why "it's a pipe dream" have probably come flooding over you. Part of examining your life is

---

7   This is known as the HAVE, DO, BE exercise and can be help people find out what they want

notes

to deal with these doubts. After all, there is some validity to your concerns—you have historical proof of what your limitations are. Write these doubts and limitations down. This is essential—they must be brought to the light of day or they will be constant naggers on you, sucking up energy.

Take out another piece of paper and write down "Why I Can't." Under this heading write down all the reasons that have foiled you so far—your financial situation, your lack of time, your physical or psychological well-being, your overwhelming responsibilities, the people in your life that drag you down either by their presence or by telling you you can't, and so on. Write them all down. Do it now.

Okay, now, you have your reasons why you cannot. And guess what? You are right about them! It should look something like this:

Why I can't

1. I'm not old enough
2. No one in my family ever has
3. It will never work
4. I've tried before
5. I will look stupid
6 My wife doesn't agree
7. I could lose alot of money
8. I'm not that type of person
9. I just can't

Think about the dynamic complaining and constantly reminding yourself of the reasons you might not succeed creates in your life. You are actually perpetuating the argument for why you cannot do it.

....

notes

How much energy is squandered by constantly thinking negatively? Picture a conversation between "Why I Can't," a historically based dog, and the future *Vision (A Total Life)*, another dog. Both of them are yapping, pay attention to me. Guess which of the two dogs will outlast and win? The one you feed the most. That dog will get stronger while the other gets weaker and less powerful. Do you want all of your reasons you can't get what you want barking at you all the time?

Got it? Perfect. Now, here is the next step. Take your list, cross it out and re-label it, like this:

Why I can't

1. I'm not old enough
2. No one in my family ever has
3. It will never work
4. I've tried before
5. I will look stupid
6 My wife doesn't agree
7. I could lose alot of money
8. I'm not that type of person
9. I just can't

....

notes

STOP SPENDING SO MUCH TIME ARGUING WHY YOU CANNOT!
CRUMPLE THIS LIST INTO A NICE BASKETBALL SHAPED PAPER BALL AND DUNK IT
INTO THE TRASH!

One of the prototypical *Total Life* success men I walk with used to be addicted to the notion that other people were responsible for his unhappiness. Everyone around him was responsible, but not him. It is no great surprise that in his marriage, he perceived that his wife was always the problem! At some point, he quit thinking, "What's wrong with my wife? Why is she so_____? If she could only_____!" Instead, he changed his thinking and re-channeled all the energy spent in blame into a possibility exploration. He started thinking, "How will I make this marriage better? What am I committed to do?"

At that point, his relationship—a relationship that *up until now* had been fraught with conflict, criticism, and degradation—became whole, fun, exciting, and brilliant. How will you do it? How will you focus on the goal instead of all the reasons it cannot happen?

What is next in the possibility exploration is actually the most important step. Take out another sheet of paper and entitle it "How I Will."

Under that heading, write down any possibilities you can conjure up or invent that will enable you to achieve the life you have *Designed*.

....

notes

Brainstorm the possibilities without making judgments about them; you can decide later which ones to hone in on. It might look something like this:

How i will

1. Call John Smith and discuss details
2. Go back to school and train
3. Develop a team around the concept
4. Pick up the phone and make calls
5. Put together a business plan
6. Run the idea by friends and family
7. Organize my calendar, block out time
8. Do research and start
9. Start reading books that will help

This chart needs to be displayed somewhere so you can see it daily. At this point you should have a *Design* and some actions that you can implement to move you toward its execution. This is all part of the first step for *Total Life* success—examining and then *designing* your life. Remember, the possibilities for your life begin and end in your mind! So keep asking yourself, "wouldn't it be nice if_____? Then set a plan in motion to make it happen. Lastly, remember it is easier to steer a moving car than a parked one so the sooner you get moving the better chance you have to get to where you want to go.

notes

IF YOU DO NOT KNOW WHERE YOU' ARE GOING,
YOU'LL END UP SOMEWHERE ELSE.

YOGI BERRA

THE JOURNEY OF A THOUSAND MILES BEGINS
WITH ONE STEP.

LAO-TZU

notes

YOU MUST HAVE LONG-RANGE GOALS TO KEEP YOU
FROM BEING FRUSTRATED BY SHORT-RANGE FAILURES.
CHARLES C. NOBLE

WHEN YOU DETERMINE WHAT YOU WANT YOU HAVE
MADE THE MOST IMPORTANT DECISION IN YOUR LIFE.
DOUGLAS LURTON

notes

VISION VS. VICE

Key concept: You will follow the direction you set.
The level of thinking that created the problem is insufficient
to solve it
Albert Einstein

Where there is no vision people cast off restraint.
Ancient Hebrew Proverb

HOW IT WORKS

Vision is the fuel of *Design*. If your *Design* were a car and a location, then *Vision* would be the gas the car needs to get you where you want to go. The problem many of us face is we create a great plan, an exciting plan, and then proceed to trap ourselves in *Vices*—things that clamp down on us and keep us from moving. To have *A Total Life*— all the intimacy, joy, money, success, legacy, fun, peace, health and more—we need to have a *Vision*, a picture if you will, of what we look like embracing all those things. Understanding our *Vices* is key to enjoying the process of life because we can only pursue our *Vision* when we come to terms with our brokenness, our weakness, and our substitutes.

Oftentimes, rather than going after what you want, you may find yourself simply running from what you do not want to face. The only problem is that we will never get what we want if *Vices* or our old choices run our lives. So what do we do? We plan, commit, and *Design* even more than we thought possible. We invest, make commitments, and risk all of our current comforts to pursue freedom from the past.

A *Vision* can come to us in many ways, we can be listening to music and bam…it hits us, or we might be asking ourselves questions about our life and choices. Sometimes a movie, a great piece of literature or a good conversation with a friend will inspire a grand *Vision* in us. Be waiting and watching for your *Vision* and passion to form, and be prepared to move toward it immediately. You will find that once you begin to pursue your *Design* with *Vision* and passion, the road will still feel a bit challenging, but you will be moving forward not backward.

....

notes

The proverb referenced at the beginning of this chapter, states a vital truth about life—when you have no vision, there is nothing to direct you, constrain you, guide you, and compel you. You simply gravitate to the path of least resistance and do whatever is immediately gratifying.

Traditionally a *Vice* is seen as some kind of moral fault, for example, drunkenness, gambling, drug use, sexual licentiousness, etc. No doubt, these are *Vices,* but let us think beyond this concept. Why do people develop *Vices?* What is it that *Vices* do? What effect do they have on people?

It is clear that people develop *Vices* in an effort to make life tolerable, combat loneliness or replace worry. Vices are escapism. Put another way, *Vices* are attempts to address what is missing from a person's life. It could be excitement, love, true comfort, or joy. Watching sports on TV might become a cheap substitute for playing and succeeding at a sport yourself. You get all the adrenalin cheering for your team, with little to none of the sacrifice, hard work, and discipline needed truly to feel those feelings. The problem, of course, is that *Vices* are cheap substitutes that cannot deliver the long-term payoff that they pretend they can. If the goal is to relax and be at peace in life, a quick fix might be to drink or smoke as a method to take the edge and stress out of life; however, those tactics used repetitively can cause major problems in other areas such as health and relationships. It may be better to *Design* into your life things such as yoga, meditation, good sex, music, a party with your friends, an occasional cocktail and other fun relaxing activities.

....

notes

Another problem with *Vices* has to do with the other common definition of *Vice*—a tool for holding. Everyone has probably seen this tool. They are strong, forged metal "jaws" that tightly grip and hold something on which you are working. That is exactly what *Vices* do to us as we walk through life. They hold us back from soaring. They keep us trapped, held back, and stuck. *Vices* have us; we do not have them.

The term *Vice* also is a prefix attached to someone who acts in the place of another or fills a vacancy, as when a vice president fills in when the office is vacated. *Vices* are like that too. They are used to fill a vacancy, and oftentimes the choices made by a vice office holder can be choices of survival ("Let's make it through this crisis") rather than choices of *Vision*. Let me explain the concept of vice in another way, because this is an important distinction. You want the president to run your life—the part of you that really has a *Vision* and cares and is determined, *the winner*—not the vice president, who simply tries to hold on while circumstances that he or she did not *Design* land in his or her path. If your *Vices* are running your life, I guarantee you are overwhelmed and simply struggling through life as the powerful negative circumstances bombard you like waves in a hurricane.

It is interesting to note that *Vices* are rather easy to form. The reason for this is that they represent the path of least resistance mentioned above. If there is nothing to constrain me, nothing to direct me, nothing that compels me, and my life is basically about feeling good or comfortable, then *Vices* are okay substitutes. They do not necessarily get me to where I want to be, but they do serve to make life tolerable, and I can get some kicks out of them. So it should be clear

notes

that if you are living with a *Vice* grip on your life and find yourself going nowhere day after day, you should go back and re-read principle one several times. Onward!

When you start *Designing* your life and creating a great plan for your life, you will find yourself going after all that you want with all the energy previously devoted to your *Vices*. Can you imagine how good you are going to feel when you pursue your *Vision* using the energy previously spent on the pursuit of your *Vices*, those short-term pain relievers?

Vision is true possibility, a fearless exploration of the infinite, like Gandhi had on his quest to change human rights in India or UCLA basketball coach John Wooden had on his quest for great basketball players; both believed in a fearless exploration of greatness.

Visionaries have a reason to make hard choices. They have a reason to put off making the quick buck and instead learn how to make millions or billions. They understand that education is needed as a platform for confidence, and do not look for the way out; they look for the way ahead. You see, only people with *Vision* will restrain themselves and accept delayed gratification.

People with *Vision* are continually guided by it. *Vision*, rather than being only a goal, is something that guides and directs. It is like the North Star. No matter where you are, if you are deciding what action to take, or if you lose your way or get sidetracked, finding the North Star can help you get back on track, and get refocused and ready to take the next step back in the direction of the goal.

It is truly unfortunate that some people *Design* their lives with a compartmentalized *Vision* so that even when they accomplish their

notes

objectives they are still empty and unsatisfied. Therefore, it is key that principle one, *Design Your Life* for *Total Life* success is accomplished. Once it has been *Designed*, I urge you to keep the *Vision* in front of you and allow the *Vices*, the cheap substitutes, to fall away like the early morning fog burning off.

The most effective *Visions* are very simple and can be accessed no matter what you are thinking or doing. Things like, I want to be happy, I always want to be improving or I want to care about everyone. Let's say your *Vision* was to have a close, intimate, loving relationship with your spouse. Let's say you have spent time imagining it, you have *Designed* it in your mind, and have committed to it. Now, when you have an opportunity to do something that would interfere with that *Design*, the *Vision* could keep you on the path that you set out to follow. You might find yourself saying no to working overtime or hanging with friends, or feel compelled to address key problems that could keep you from that close, intimate, loving relationship. Again if the *design* is a location *vision* is the fuel.

Ask yourself what would be a *Vision* compelling enough for you to interrupt the chronic tendencies that have prevented you from having *Total Life* success? Perhaps you have not ever allowed yourself to really dream about what life could look like for you. Perhaps you decided, or were taught, that the best you could do in life was survive. If so, then you probably settled for crumbs, never even considering that a banquet is available to you.

Let us take few moments now to determine whether you have been living more from *Vision* or from *Vice*.

notes

FIVE HUNDRED MILLION DOLLAR EXERCISE

Imagine yourself sitting in front of the TV on another typical night, after another typical day at work. Dinner is over and you want to unwind. Not able to find any intriguing programming, you have been channel surfing for a while when a particular program catches your eye long enough to cause you to put the remote down. Between commercials, the official Lotto drawing comes on.

You have been buying a lottery ticket once a week for about ten years. You have taken in the ads hook, line, and sinker, which state, "You can't win if you don't play." You have justified the long-shot odds by spending only a buck each week. The numbers chosen have always been the same—a combination of birthdays, anniversaries, and that "lucky" number you had on a uniform in high school.

As the ping-pong balls float up and the beautiful announcer reads the numbers, you realize that they sound vaguely familiar. Of course, the excitement of following along with your ticket in hand dissipated about two weeks into the process, so you are only halfway paying attention. The last number read is that "lucky" one. Intrigued, you sit up, lean forward, and read the numbers more intently. The first one is one of the birthdays and the second is the anniversary. One by one, you read and recognize the numbers. Your heart starts to palpitate and you incredulously toy with the idea that you have successfully chosen every number. Grabbing a note pad nearby you jot down the numbers. Not trusting your memory, you begin to rummage about for the Lotto ticket…"Where is it?" Suddenly, you find the ticket,

notes

read the numbers, and sure enough, they match! Imagine now all the emotions and thoughts that would begin coursing through you. Not only have you won, but also the next day you discover that you were the only winner and the jackpot is five hundred million dollars. You may be saying to yourself, "I do not need five hundred million dollars," but this is not about needing anything.

This exercise will add value to your life if you are already worth a billion dollars or if you have negative net worth. The idea is not about money, it is about possibility, responsibility, clarity, options, and more. So even if you do not need the money, forge on into the exercise. You will be glad you did.

To get the best results from this book, it is important to do this exercise on paper and not just in your head. So get out a sheet of paper and something with which to write. Now, imagine yourself in the above situation, and write down exactly what you are going to do in the next:

- Minute
- Ten minutes
- Two hours
- 1st day
- 5 days
- 15 days
- 1st month
- 6 months
- 1st year
- 5 years

Close the book now and write these things down.

notes

Now you should have the sheet in hand. If you did not do the exercise, put the book down and do it now. You will not receive the benefit until you can see what you wrote down.

- What was your first thought?
- What thoughts were racing through your mind?
- Did it simply feel like more work for you, more responsibility?
- What was your first feeling?
- Whom do you call first? Why?
- Do you tell them everything?
- Do you notice suspicion rising up in you?
- Were you so excited you did something silly, funny, crazy?
- Did you just go into shock?
- Does this sudden wealth flush up distrust—even with people who only moments ago you completely trusted?

Let us look more closely at this last response. If you found yourself not trusting those you trusted only moments ago, this could be projection in action—a conversation within yourself that identifies the expectation you would have if one of your friends won that much money—maybe to be set-up by them, or at least gifted a good amount because, after all, they do not need that much. Or, maybe your friends or family are not very good with money and you know deep down their advice would not help you with your new *Vision*. . Or, maybe your friends or family are very controlling when it comes to money and have their own ideas about what your Vision should be.

··

notes

- Did you tell your spouse immediately or entertain thoughts that now you can leave her/him?
- Is the money a way out of something you should have been free of years ago, if not for your *scarcity thinking*[8]?
- Are you planning something unethical? Evil? Without judging yourself, consider honestly of what you considered doing.
- Are you going to get plastic surgery? Get Healthy? Eat Better?
- Are you going to do nothing as if nothing has changed?

In the introduction, I mentioned that money is often held up as the answer to all life's problems. I reject that idea, and you probably know of many cases that prove that belief to be false. What is inescapable, though, is how many areas money touches—how broad and sweeping its impact is on our total well being. To minimize money is like minimizing something vital, like oxygen. It is true; money cannot make you happy, cannot give you true love, and cannot create peace, joy, contentment, or humor. No, money cannot wipe away tears, sing a beautiful song, or solve issues of immortality and spirituality. But, what it can do is so rare and so unique that nothing can replace it. That is why ignoring it is one of the most problematic mental failures in human existence. It is problematic to overvalue money, but it is also unwise to misinterpret its use or value.

---

8   See Glossary

....

notes

How does this relate to *Vision*? One of the biggest fears—global, life restricting fears—is "scarcity," the fear that there is not enough. And certainly one of the most common fears is THE FEAR OF NOT HAVING ENOUGH MONEY!

I know a person very well whose net worth is in the fifty million plus range. He has had this money for over twenty-five years and yet he lives in a house with no electricity or running water, wears clothes bought from charity stores, and is a veritable hermit.. Now, you may quickly write him off as mentally challenged and say he should be institutionalized, but if you were to talk to him, you would find him pretty coherent. But one thing is for sure, he has a scarcity mindset. It is safe to say that for him he will never have enough money. Too often, money falsely represents time, possibility, freedom, hope, and security.

Sometimes the lack of money is produced by the *scarcity mindset*— the fear of not being enough or having enough, and then living as if that were true. In contrast, the mindset that produces wealth is one of *abundance*, which refers to the certainty that there is more than enough and that all one needs to do is become *aware* of how to get it.. Consider, if you are not living in some ways, today, as if you have millions of dollars, YOU WILL PROBABLY NEVER HAVE IT. By "living as if you have it," I do not mean living "high off the hog" and spending up to the limits on all your credit cards. I mean having the relationships, goals, mindset, and discipline required to produce and sustain that kind of money[9]. Specifically, you should understand such concepts as tax planning, estate planning, investment planning, real

---

9   See Glossary

estate, insurance, cash flow management, liability issues, and so on. What's interesting is understanding these concepts before you need them actually helps you go about attaining the wealth you want. It's like a person who pays a trainer to give him health advice before he is healthy. The advice comes before the person gets in shape. Understanding, becoming *aware* and education are huge key components to attaining *A Total Life*.

If we asked Donald Trump or Bill Gates to do this exercise they would know exactly who to call, what to say, what the plan would be, and would feel totally comfortable with the new responsibility, not overwhelmed or overly excited. They both know that the marginal utility of a dollar decreases as you earn more income. Put more simply, the more dollars you have, the less the last dollar helps you. Put even more simply, if you have zero dollars and someone gives you one thousand dollars, that money feels life saving and transformational. If you have a billion dollars and you receive one thousand dollars, you almost do not even notice. The money has less value to you.

There is no *holy grail*[10]for the visionary, only implementation and execution. Real visionaries, who may not even have any money, would not be surprised by the extra funds; they would simply implement the strategy already developed years prior. However, the *scarcity thinkers*[11], rather than hitting the ground running, would have to get up to speed and may be forced to rely on others with whom they do not have relationships.

---

10   See glossary
11   See glossary

....

notes

To circle back to a previous example, consider that some of us think like this: "If I had a tank full of gas I would take my car some-where" instead of like this, "I want to go to Paris, Africa, New York, and the Bahamas, but don't have the funds, so I am going to find a way to get the resources to go." Planning before you have the resources creates the appropriate conviction so that if the resources come, they are integrated appropriately. If you plan only after you have the funds, you are never really sure if those things are things you really wanted to do, things you are willing to sacrifice for, or just nice things you can do now.

Another way to think about this is to recognize that every person is already moving towards a particular outcome in terms of how pre-pared they would be if they realized *Total Life* success. The way you are currently living (your *Design*) is setting you on a certain trajectory towards certain outcomes. Every day, the little choices we make either veer us towards a destination consistent with what we say we want, or towards another destination that is miles away from what we long for. We are dictating, in no uncertain terms, future outcomes by present choices…and have been doing this all along.

CHRONIC VS. ACUTE

The word "chronic" can be defined as follows: constant; habitual; continuing a long time or recurring frequently; having long had a disease, habit, weakness, or the like. The word "acute" can be defined as follows: sharp or severe in effect; intense, extremely great or seri-

....
notes

ous; crucial; critical, immediate, or impulsive. Another way to think about chronic versus acute is to think about the concept of "geometric progression" or the "rule of 72." The rule of 72 is a financial term used to estimate the growth of one's investments over time. The rules states that if you take the interest rate you are getting on your money and divide it by 72, your money will double by the quotient. For example, if you had one hundred thousand dollars invested at 10 percent return, based on the rule of 72, your money would double in 7.2 years. Therefore, in 7.2 years, your one hundred thousand would be worth two hundred thousand dollars. This concept also works in the negative. If you borrowed one hundred thousand dollars at 10 percent, you would owe two hundred thousand in 7.2 years.

Further Explanation

$72/10 = 7.2$

In 7.2 years, your money will double at 10 percent return.

One hundred thousand dollars in 7.2 years will be two hundred thousand.

I believe, just as with money, a person's life, their character, is also shaped over time, both positively and negatively. I would go so far as to say that if you were an impatient person, over time that impatience would only get worse. At some point, there will be few acute solutions to fix the problem of impatience. I would not go so far as to say that you have become incurably impatient, but more that it would take a great deal of effort and time to turn around that long-term chronic behavior. At the same time if you have become and chosen peace for your life over a long period of time, there is probably very few acute problems that will derail your peaceful demeanor and spirit. The same

notes

goes for your health. We have all seen friends who simply gain a few pounds a year for a while, and then all of a sudden four pounds a year times ten years equals forty pounds overweight. Our chronic behaviors are sneaky and the outcomes are not seen over night; rather, they are revealed later on when the symptoms finally catch up with our actions. It is so important to have a *Design* for your health so that you can intentionally make all those good, small choices you need to facilitate a long-term health.

The present state of our lives has been created by the choices we have made along the way. Our successes and problems are created over time by those daily choices. Our thinking produces our choices. As shown by the examples of lottery winners, and other people who seem to recreate similar results over and over again, the problems people have are usually the outcome of the mindsets that produced them. Furthermore, simply applying an acute remedy does not necessarily fix them. So often, up to 75 percent of the time, lottery winners will lose all of their winnings and end up even worse than they were when they started. **Wealth is not just money; it is a combination of *whom you know, how you feel, what you know, and what you have.*** I will review this in the next chapter in more detail.

While acute remedies may remedy a problem temporarily, they cannot permanently fix a problem that has been created by chronic choices. If the thinking that has created the problem in the first place is not changed, the acute remedy will only temporarily address whatever is off base. Without the change in thinking, a person will always revert back to the chronic behavior that caused the problem in the first place. Therefore, to have *Total Life* success necessitates changing

....

notes

the thinking that produced the behaviors that have undermined your success to date.

The important thing to recognize in all this is that it is imperative to give yourself a break! If your life is the way it is as a result of consistent action (or inaction), then it follows that to change it will also take consistent action. You must therefore extend yourself *grace*. Beating yourself up adds nothing to the fabric of *A Total Life*. Just simply make some adjustments, head down the new path, and enjoy the new view you have created for yourself—the future *Vision* about which you are excited.

STAY THE COURSE

Once you have *Designed* a life for total success, it would be disastrous if you gave up in the first two hours of your journey because it was just too hard. This is why understanding the difference between chronic and acute problems is so important. You have to give yourself time to realize your *Vision*. The journey must be enjoyed, loved, because it is a long one and the process really is the destination. If you have been living through a broken, dysfunctional *Vision* for twenty years, yet expect to change overnight, you are guaranteed to perceive failure. It would be similar to getting on a plane to China and at the last minute deciding you want to land in Europe and then being disappointed when you land. It takes time to change direction and set a new course.

notes

It is a delicate balance, however, because you may need some acute, quick movement right now for example, you may need to, as they say, "stop the bleeding." If you want to be a financial success and healthy, you may want to immediately stop going into debt and start eating healthier. While the actual results may not immediately change, the trajectory you are on can change immediately. What we do today can drastically alter the long-term results. As pointed out by Malcolm Gladwell in his book, *The Tipping Point*, the dynamic of geometric progression is a reality and can become like a virus that spreads through your whole life like an epidemic. Geometric Progression is what takes over when a news story, new toy (remember Tickle Me Elmo?), new fashion item, or new band seems to come out of nowhere and becomes ubiquitous.

GEOMETRIC PROGRESSION

Geometric progression is what transpired when a wave of anti-crime sentiment swept through New York and transformed the city from a place people feared going to at night to a city that saw its crime rate rapidly plummet in a very short time. What is interesting to note is that this wave in New York began by tackling relatively minor crimes such as graffiti and subway gate jumping (the action whereby passengers of NY's subways would jump over the turnstiles without paying). As these more minor crimes were successfully addressed, the bigger crimes started to decline. This can also happen in your life.

notes

By making small changes you can end up with sweeping, brilliant results.

We tend to expect output to be linearly proportional to input. For example, imagine a sheet of paper folded in half and then in half again, and so on for fifty folds. Most would expect the thickness to be about the size of a big dictionary or perhaps as tall as a refrigerator. But Gladwell suggests the geometric progression would make the thickness more like the distance between the earth and the sun. Another example is that of the growth of the dollar. If you double the size of one dollar you have two dollars, an additional one dollar, but if you double the size of 50 million you have 50 million more dollars. The same percentage growth on a higher value of dollars creates drastic and even shocking results. At some point the paper begins doubling at drastic rates as the last few folds are doubling a greater thickness. That is how life can be, sometimes when we start a project or a goal the results do not show up for a long time and then all of a sudden from what seems to be out of nowhere, major accomplishments start coming in and all that you have worked so hard for is realized. Here is one more example of the progressive effect of goals. If you set out to build an amusement park so much time, energy, creativity and execution is needed before the idea becomes an actuality. Imagine if 4 months before the completion of the project the developer or owner simply stopped because the project was taking too long or becoming too difficult or expensive. Although that sounds crazy many of us do that in our lives, we work months or years on a relationship, idea, or health goal only to stop just moments, days or months before the actualization of our goal.

....

notes

One can easily see this concept manifest in their finances. If someone was to begin saving even 10 percent of every dollar they made from the time they were twenty years old, getting only a marginal return, they would easily be millionaires by the time they retired. That is the good news about geometric progression. The bad news is that chronic problems, problems that have been long term, are not completely changed by acute actions. Many people live a life eating food that creates major health problems only to one day try and reverse the effects with a single surgery or single fad diet. Often these people get the short term results they want only to fall back into the same patterns that created the problem in the first place. Again, this is why grace is required and why you must change what you are thinking and doing today. You must not be to demanding on yourself as you begin to change what you are doing with your life because it took years even generations to get where you are currently at and yet if you want different results the sooner you can change what you think about the sooner you will be changing long term negative habits and giving yourself a chance to live a full powerful life.

Consequently, if you were to happen into unearned wealth by way of inheritance or by hitting a jackpot—and up until then not lived a life congruent with someone who is setting themselves up for living a life of wealth and influence—you are likely to end up squandering what you get. Not having earned the money, it may be easier to flitter it away especially if the first thing you may is start spending to make up for lost time. Because of a lack of *Vision* and education, some people will fuel their addictions and find themselves in Vegas or with fast cars and unnecessary material objects. There is nothing wrong with

....

notes

nice things that inspire you and others, but a person with *Vision* has educated themselves in order to know the time, place, and order in which to make such purchases.

STOP GAP TECHNIQUE

What will make you feel so great right now is to *Design* a "Vice Management System" (VMS). This system will enable you quickly to stop the thinking that can create bad feelings and emotional discontentment. The best system I have ever come across is from one of my mentors, author of *Burning Desire*, Doran Andre. Here is how it works. Whenever you are feeling like your actions or feelings are not congruent with the future you desire, you yell, "STOP," or internally yell, "STOP!" Right after you stop, you should begin to think about every great action, event, or feeling you have ever had. For example, you might think about your first kiss, getting your driver's license, winning in sports, graduating from school, or meeting the man or woman of your dreams. The more great "anchors" that you can connect with the better, so really try to remember all the best times in your life. Once all these feelings and memories come rushing over you, it is now time to re-engage in your current life with the new feelings that have arisen from reflecting on great moments from your past.

When this technique is practiced over and over again, it will become so much a part of your life that you will begin to notice that the time between bad actions and feelings to positive actions and feelings will decrease until you are truly living completely out of *Vision*.

notes

Here is another important question to ask yourself, "Is your *Vision* bigger than your *Vices?*" You may discover that you are currently living out of *Vice* rather than *Vision*. There is no *Design* good enough to make up for a life of *Vices*. *Vices* kill *Vision* and possibility and render even the greatest of persons powerless.

I have already mentioned some of the bolder visionaries in history. We could go on and on with more examples and yet always find very similar ingredients—intrepid souls willing to challenge conventional wisdom, delay gratification, reframe failure, make requests, and not substitute their *Vision* for a *Vices*.

It is important to point out that people who are living out of purpose and *Vision* are currently enjoying the process of succeeding as well as the success itself and are not merely frantically looking for the proverbial Holy Grail. The Holy Grail represents that elusive answer to all of life's problems. Some people spend their entire life chasing after it and consequently neglect the day-to-day choices that actually move them towards the life they really desire. Many people who live in scarcity are looking for the Holy Grail because they have mistakenly convinced themselves that it will help them, that it is the answer, but the fact of the matter is that no amount of money can fix a life you have behaved into or *Designed* yourself. **Happiness does not come from a windfall but from a life of good choices.**

As you may have seen in the exercise about winning the lottery, one of the main problems is that people live and choose in the **present** in ways that are incongruent with the **future** they say they want. They do not establish the relationships necessary to set that future up

....

notes

and they put off setting up the needed infrastructure required to live *A Total Life*. Instead, they imagine that when their ship comes in, or when they find their Holy Grail, they will shift into the lifestyle they say they want.

This thinking goes something like this: "I'll find an estate planner when I get enough money." "When I'm not so stressed financially, I'll be able to exercise and get healthy." "When I have the money I need, I will begin to eat healthy." (It costs so much to do so, you know). "When I am in a better position financially, I can begin contributing to charity." "When my financial concerns are resolved then I'll begin enjoying quality family time."

These statements have many variations, but what they all have in common is that the life one longs for will begin when _____ (you fill in the blank) happens. The people who make these types of statements are contrasted with those who are already engaging in the life they desire at some level. The real difference is that people who are not looking for the Holy Grail usually have a high level of peace and contentment and tend to enjoy the process as well as the destination. In addition, they tend to have less fear of failure and have high expectations for what is possible for themselves.

Why do so many people give up on going for their dreams? Why do many of us sit back and wait to win the lottery rather than make and earn our own victories? It is because the path to success or greatness is tricky in that no one solution will work for everyone. There is no quick fix, simple solution to having your dream life now. Many times, we just get frustrated and give up on our dreams, settle back

notes

....

down with our current comforts, and reconcile for a reasonable life. The next principle, *Integration*, will help you discover how you can break down some of the complexity, work on what you can control, and move forward toward your goals and dreams, even when you are tired, frustrated, and overwhelmed.

notes

JUST AS SOON AS PEOPLE MAKE ENOUGH MONEY
TO LIVE COMFORTABLY, THEY WANT TO LIVE
EXTRAVAGANTLY.

ANONYMOUS

TO ACCOMPLISH GREAT THINGS, WE MUST NOT ONLY
ACT, BUT ALSO DREAM, NOT ONLY PLAN, BUT ALSO
BELIEVE.

ANATOLE FRANCE

notes

MAN CANNOT BE SATISFIED WITH MERE SUCCESS.
HE IS CONCERNED WITH THE TERMS UPON WHICH
SUCCESS COMES TO HIM.
CHARLES A BENNETT

THERE IS A TIME FOR EVERYTHING.
THOMAS EDISON

notes

INTEGRATION

*Key concept: True power to achieve Total Life success
is in Integration.
Indeed, our world is an interconnected
web of relationships.*
O'Murchu

Everything is connected to everything else.
The First Law of Ecology

HOW IT WORKS

How does *Integration* fit in to the pursuit for *A Total Life?* What is *Integration* all about? *Integration* is, what one might call, the grace factor in all this. In other words, we have a *Design* for our life, and we have a *Vision* propelling us to joy, peace, wealth, connectedness, health, serenity, fun, passion, intimacy, *A Total Life*, and more. Sometimes, a wonderful life just seems to continually elude us, and experiencing that life seems almost impossible. The question emerges then, "Do we give up on the exciting endeavor?" And the answer is NO. In this next chapter about *Integration* you will begin to understand how all the ingredients fit together to make *A Total life*. Think about what a chef goes through to make the perfect meal. He or she has to take into consideration all the ingredients needed and the timing of putting it all together in addition to the temperature, presentation, and environment, and it all has to happen seamlessly so as to look effortless to the lucky person who gets to enjoy the masterpiece. The chef's genius is the perfect *Integration* of all the parts and variables to create an extraordinary meal. *Integration* is bringing things together for a common cause or purpose unlike balance, which is more focused on a commitment not to be too focused on one thing.

What is *Integration?* Think about all we have in our minds and in our worlds—thoughts like "Are we enough?" "What do our friends think?" "Are we doing it right?" "What about our health?" "Can we sleep?" "Are we good?" "Should we?" "Could we?" "Why don't we?" "Who should we be?" "Why?" "When will we feel ok?" "Why can't we just...?" "What if?" "Are we happy?" "Should we be?" "Should

....

notes

we laugh?" "At what?" "What about our finances?" "Are we giving enough?" "Do we need to start saving?" "Are we good parents?" "Do we need to be successful?" "What is successful?" Our past can haunt us and the future can scare us. Taxes, bills, cars, clothes, and so on, keep us busy without growing or learning—just busy. We do not want to plan and we do not want regrets. Some people do not like us; others love us. We want to do bad things, and we want to feel good. All of this and more might be running through our head at any moment, and that is why more than anything else we need GRACE, to be easy on ourselves, and let ourselves grow and learn at a comfortable pace in an imperfect manner. That is, for these purposes, the goal of this principle, *Integration*. *Integration* is putting all the pieces together with joy and contentment, with ease and poise, developing a grand dream or *Vision* through the *Integration* of hundreds of concepts, principles, and activities all toward your grand visionary *Design*. It is about an easy, relaxed, fun stewardship of time.

Where does power come from? Where do some get the energy to accomplish more in one year than others can accomplish in a lifetime? How is it that some people seem to succeed with what looks to be effortless grace and poise? **Consider** Michael Jordan, who, with his timing, style, and touch made the winning, last-second shot against the Utah Jazz in game six of the 1998 playoffs seem almost scripted.

If I told you the answer to having that kind of Michael Jordan like success was as easy as taking a pill once a day, everyone would do it. Some people search all over the globe for pills that will help them lose weight, get more energy, sleep better, have a stronger sex drive, and even be happier. The pharmaceutical industry is booming because so many people are looking for the quick fix, the simple solution.

The problem is that taking a pill is like telling a golfer, whose golf game is in the one hundreds, to keep his arm straight on the back swing as the only solution. In other words, there is no simple, easy, quick-fix solution to a horrible golf game, just like there is no easy solution to fixing problems that took years to create. Imagine if a golfer asked his coach for some advice as to how he could hit the ball farther and the coach simply responded "swing harder." We know that the real answer is a complex *Integration* of hundreds of factors that must be worked on individually and combined into a total solution, consistently. Imagine being committed to improving your golf swing and the only thing you did was curls at the gym in order to develop bigger biceps. A great golf swing is a fluid *Integration* of body, mind, and spirit. The body needs to be both powerful and flexible and the mind keen and focused, not only on the ball itself, but also with an

....

notes

eye on where you want the ball to go, calibrating the force of the swing to achieve the goal and not over or under shooting. Finally, the spirit must be calm and quiet, able to handle/withstand the pressure. Real power is realized only when all of these factors are in sync. A good golfer makes it look simple, but it is really not, as those of us who have tried the sport can attest. It is important to notice that balance is not the goal, yet it is one component in having a good golf swing. Balance is not *Integration*.

To attain the life you dream of, there is no quick fix, no magic pill, only a path of trial and error, working diligently on all the components until soon you find yourself fluidly enjoying all life has to offer. I once read something that used the acronym, K.I.S.S., which stands for, "Keep It Simple Stupid." The idea behind this acronym is that many people make winning or success so complicated that they cannot stay focused, lose sight of the actual goal, and just get buried under details. While keeping it simple is generally advantageous, I have found that many use simplification as an excuse for poor thinking and over-compartmentalization.

Think about a car engine. Is that a simple concept? Think about the human heart. Is that a simple concept? Think about an uncut diamond; is it not the facets that make it beautiful and the precision cuts that make it shine? Oftentimes, our greatest achievements and most revered concepts, products, and ideas are complicated in nature and have been put together with meticulous precision—and are executed with very exacting timing and *Integration* of all the components. Imagine that you are a diamond. Now think about all the cuts you want to make so you can shine.

notes

In some way, there is a power or winner pill concept that one can take to win in life and that is to un-compartmentalize, or, put more positively, to *Integrate*. Some people think that to win in life, to succeed, they just have to be good at one thing, like basketball, finances, or relationships, but success in one compartment does not equal success in life. The definition of *Integration*, according to Webster's is "The state of combination or the process of combining into completeness and harmony" Oftentimes, we succeed, but the success does not harmoniously fit into our lives; rather, it can sometimes ruin or become a detriment. An example of this is when a movie star finally hits it big and achieves success in the eyes of society and all of his or her peers, but yet only moments, months, or a year later finds his or herself in depression, on drugs, making horrible decisions, completely unraveled, or even sometimes deceased. Success without *Integration* to an overall concept of peace, joy, happiness, love, and the like may not be success at all.

One man who is walking in *Total Life* success described *Integration* in a very unique way. To him, *Integration* is being absolutely and completely content, while being fully committed to pursuing who he must become, in every sphere of his life. You see, that is another aspect of *Integration*, being fully present and content where you are, while still allowing all the possibilities to be available, and not becoming discontented or jaded with your current situation. Eckhart Tolle, author of THE POWER OF NOW, describes this state of being in his book beautifully. Your ability to be present at all times propels you toward your future. One moment at a time.

....

notes

The concept of *Integration*, as it is being used in this book can sometimes feels a bit mystic, intriguing, and paradoxical. For Example, John Wooden, one of the most successful college basketball coaches ever, once told his players, "Be quick, but not in a hurry." I bring this up because oftentimes, to get the life we want necessitates acting in a way that is counter to what we are used to doing. Like being quick, but not in a hurry gives us the opportunity to work at a rapid pace without getting out of control—sometimes we may need to be focused while open to the best possibilities. What I am trying to do is explain more about *Integration* in a way that you will become more convinced that to have *A Total Life* will necessitate having a great *Design*, being a visionary, and putting it all together (*Integrating*), in such a way that you marshal all your resources, time, and creativity into a complex, integrated way that enables you to experience the *Total Life* you and I want. Remember, life is kind of like the golf swing, complicated but not impossible.

EXAMINE WATER/EXAMINE YOUR LIFE

Mr. Emoto is a Japanese scientist who has been studying water molecules for decades. From Mr. Emoto's work, we are provided with factual evidence, that human vibrational energy, thoughts, words, ideas, and music, affect the molecular structure of water, the very same water that comprises over 70 percent of a mature human body and covers the same amount of our planet. Mr. Emoto has been visually

notes

documenting these molecular changes in water by means of his photographic techniques. He freezes droplets of water and then examines them under a dark field microscope that has photographic capabilities. His work clearly demonstrates the diversity of the molecular structure of water and the effect of the environment upon the structure of the water. It is so amazing because words like love, joy, hope, and Mother Theresa as well as Beethoven's music create beautiful snowflake like structures, while hate, anger, Hitler, and heavy metal music create broken very ugly type structures. Just as relationships with your friends affect your health and your connection to God or spirituality can affect the wealth you accumulate over your lifetime, your thoughts can affect the molecular structure of water. Everything is working together; we are all *Integrated*.

What is true about the interconnectedness in all things in our material universe is true within ourselves as well and applies to all the aspects that comprise *Designing* the life for which you long. What I am arguing, in other words, is that achievement in one aspect of life (such as finances or romance) without success in another aspect (such as leaving the legacy you desire or your health) is really not success at all.

The concept of *Integration* suggests that things may not be as they seem. In order to have a better marriage, one may need to eat better. In order to lose weight, one may need to reconcile with their father. To be a great business leader, one may need to go to marriage counseling. A friend of mine came to me a few years ago seeking advice about creating wealth and developing a business idea further. He had tried every possible solution, but it was not until I recommended he look to reconcile some issue he had with his father that he was able to

....

notes

break through to the next level of business success. All of life's factors intersect, thus finding creative solutions that do not always seem directly relevant to your present problems is key to achieving *Total Life* success. Success in one department, it turns out, is related to success in other areas.

TRADE-OFFS

What does it mean to have *Total Life* success? Does anyone really go for it all? Where do we find someone who is actually going for it all and living *Total Life* success?

Consider who is teaching most of us to win in life. In today's society, we have few models of total success. Could it be that we are quietly encouraged to revere and even admire those who simply win in one area of life? Because we do not have these models, it could be possible that you are making concessions, but only because you are not *Aware* of the possibility for overall success.

Marilyn Monroe, for instance, was remarkably beautiful, had an amazing personality, and a wonderful knack for performing, and yet she tragically committed suicide. Many great business leaders are praised for early success only later to be convicted of fraud, inappropriate sexual behavior, or alcohol and drug abuse. Many professional athletes seem to win on the playing field and lose in business or in their personal lives. Even some of the greatest pastors and clergyman of our day have ruined their careers and lives through deceit or unethical financial maneuvers. The examples go on and on and transcend every

notes

profession and every kind of person. These men and women seem to have had a belief that allowed them to pursue a specific goal while neglecting key elements for happiness, joy, and complete success. It is almost as if the goal becomes a way to neglect and to escape the difficult process of discovering what life is all about. The goal becomes a distraction from finding happiness, and a substitute for thinking and developing a great life. Not to overuse the golf analogy, but...hitting a 350-yard drive does not mean that you have a great golf game.

Why is it so hard to find a model of total success—a healthy, funny, creative, financially intelligent, giving, communicative, helpful, talented person who also has sound and fulfilling relationships? One reason is that we have been taught by our parents, teachers, maybe even society to make trade-offs. Statements like the following have pervaded our discussions about life:

"I may not be wealthy, but I'm happy."
"I may not be healthy, but I make a lot of money and my family comes first."
"They might have fame and fortune, but their family life is ridden with turmoil and resentment."
"We are not the closest family, but we are all successful."
"I may not be happy, but I don't hurt others and I'm a good person."
"I may not have a lot of money, but I have great friends."

Many of these conversations are about rationalizations, comparisons and creative ways of settling for bad and calling it good. People do not want to feel less than others, so rather than raise the standard

....

notes

of what is possible for themselves they lower the standard by making truly damaging trade-offs. They compartmentalize. What trade-offs might you be making? Consider how you feel about you. I wonder if maybe we bring others down or minimize their strengths so we feel more okay about ourselves.

What if I told you that all the trade-offs are irrelevant and not needed? What if it was possible to have success in every area of life that mattered? What if you could live an *Integrated* life where you were successful in every area? I believe this is possible and have written this book to support you in your quest for *Total Life* success.

The reason we do not see more people going for it **all** is because when people encounter the inevitable difficulties and challenges, most just throw in the towel and settle for a modicum of success, making trade-offs. "All" is defined in this book as a high level of success in relation to wealth, health, relationships, spirituality, social connection, education, intellectual growth, emotional strength, and peace. The select few who do not follow the trade-off path are left to navigate in nearly empty waters with only the compass of their *Vision* directing them. The fact that there is no sign of land does not bother these intrepid voyagers because they realize *A Total Life* is not a destination, a physical place where they can cross the sea and achieve their goal, but it is a continual journey and an attitude about what is possible. As they reach a particular horizon, they set of on another one and continue living life at full speed and going for it with all they have.

All this is not to say you will not identify and concentrate on a few or even one main thing in life at times. I am not talking about trying

notes

to be the best at everything. I am saying that *A Total Life* is a way of living that integrates rather than compartmentalizes all the elements that go into making life successful.

When you see your life as an *Integrated* whole, the compartmentalized mindset, which is really about justifying and compensating for what is not working, gets interrupted. Although this approach **forces** you to face what is not working, and is therefore not necessarily comfortable, the result of working with the *Integrated* whole is deep satisfaction, relational and physical health, and an overall purpose and joy in life. The reason you will feel better is that you will be dreaming again. Like a child dreaming to be a professional athlete. The dream, not the actualization of the dream, creates so much excitement and hope. **We need to have a dream if we want to have a dream come true**. Compartmentalization kills the dream because some individuals no longer go for it all, but simply go for the predictable.

The Bicycle

Fully achieving *A Total Life* necessitates *Integrating* bottom-line and top-line components. As previously stated, bottom-line components include such things as investments, retirement, tax-saving strategies, real estate optimization, health/life insurance, inheritance issues, and so on. Top-line components include purpose, *Vision*, legacy, and so on. Being deficient in either area will prevent you from living life to the fullest. The journey of life calls us to move consistently forward. Let us look at what is required in order to "roll along" in life.

Imagine life as a journey that we move through by utilizing a vehicle. Let us liken the vehicle that we use to a bicycle. The two wheels of the bike represent the two different aspects of life we have been talking about, with the back wheel symbolizing the bottom-line and the front wheel corresponding to the top-line.

The Bicycle

....

notes

Both wheels are necessary in order to achieve the results you desire. The bottom-line components provide the means for you to move **forward**; they provide the power. It is important to realize that this is a critical aspect to accomplishing what you desire in life. Consider what it is like to want to bring about certain results, but you do not have the means to do so? If that has never been the case for you, imagine if it were so now. What would it be like if you had *Vision* but no capital, no connections, no leverage to bring your *Vision* to fruition?

On the other hand, you may have all the power and wealth to complete your life *Vision*—money, business acumen, retirement accounts, and so on; yet still, you may find yourself aimlessly wandering in circles or ending up where you did not really want to be because you lack top-line clarity. The top-line components provide the **direction**; they channel and focus the power of the bottom-line elements. For example, if money were like water, *Vision* would be the hose. *Vision* directs the resources where you want them to go. Think of the incredible power that is created through this kind of conduit. The top-line components provide the channel, direction, and focus for the bottom-line power, money, and water to flow.

On the next page, there is an exercise that will help you gauge how well rounded your vehicle is. Simply be truthful and rate each sphere on both the top-line and bottom-line wheels. After you have found a number on each of the spokes, play connect the dots and you will see how you are rolling in life.

....

notes

The Bicycle

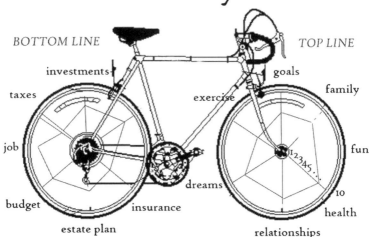

BOTTOM LINE   *TOP LINE*

investments   goals

taxes   family

exercise

job   fun

dreams

budget   insurance

estate plan   relationships   health

WEAKEST LINK

The different components that make up top-line and bottom-line concerns are like systems. Everything is interconnected like a web, whereby one strand affects another, and ultimately the whole web. Not only that, but also because everything is interconnected, by looking at an individual strand you can begin to isolate the dynamics that need to be addressed in order to transform the whole network of systems. This is because **the way you are with the one is the way you are**

....

notes

with the many. Another way of putting this is to say that if you very rigorously analyze any one component (the weakest one) of your life, like your health, and you analyze it very, very closely, paying attention to every small detail and nuance, so much about all your other areas can be revealed. Interestingly enough, by examining your weakest areas you can quickly come to terms with overriding themes that may be holding you back from success in other areas.

Now I would like to talk to you about balance. In many ways, trying to achieve balance for balance's sake is probably not a good idea. Continuing to use the bicycle analogy, imagine if your main purpose for having a well-engineered bike was simply so that you could sit on it and balance without going anywhere. Sure it may look impressive, but so what. There is an aspect to what we have been talking about that incorporates balance (no trade-offs, *Integration*, and so on.), but these aspects are not for their own sake, they are in order to accomplish a *Vision*.

Frankly, sometimes we need to focus in an **unbalanced** way for a while on certain aspects of our lives and take a break from others. For example, a sabbatical from work may be warranted when family dynamics require it. Sometimes you must focus all your energy, not just part of it, on one area for a season to get the results you want. For example if you were a fisherman and had been out at sea fishing for a few days, but there were no fish biting, even though you worked your hardest to catch them. Truly, you did everything you could to catch those fish until finally your body was tired, fatigue set in, and you were discouraged. Now just at the point when you are about to

notes

give up and go to bed, a school of giant tuna come through and you and your crew realize that the fish are biting now. At this point, balance is not the goal. You simply put balance aside and **fish as hard as you can while the fish are biting**. So many of us miss great opportunities because right at the moment we are needed to show up, we do not. When you have a clear *Vision*, like catching fish, nothing will get in the way of executing on the opportunity when it comes. So get clear and get ready because for each of us, our time, our fish, is coming.

Integration may be about putting it all together in a way that works for you and helps you implement your *Design*. No one's path will look exactly like yours, simply working harder may have worked for someone else, but you may need to relax more. Some people may have found their dreams by staying in perfect health, but your path may involve a season where your health is not the premier personal agenda. Your life and the way you *Integrate* it to get what you want is your story. Just make sure you are marshalling all of your resources in the most creative ways possible to achieve the day-to-day joy peace and passion you want.

This is what someone would say who was committed to the concept of *Integration*, "I will never be so irresponsible as to let my bottom-line issues kill my top-line possibilities. I will never let my bottom-line success allow me to forget why I spend time on bottom-line issues. I will not be a bicycle with no front tire or a bicycle with no back tire."

Now I am going to introduce the final principle, *Awareness*. The research and discovery phase of the pursuit for *A Total Life*.

....

notes

DO NOT SQUANDER TIME, FOR THAT IS
THE STUFF LIFE IS MADE OF.
BENJAMIN FRANKLIN

SUCCESS IS A JOURNEY NOT A DESTINATION.
H. TOM COLLARD

notes

ONE WHO NEVER ASKS EITHER KNOWS
EVERYTHING OR NOTHING!
MALCOLM FORBES

NO MAN REALLY BECOMES A FOOL UNTIL
HE STOPS ASKING QUESTIONS.
CHARLES P. STEINMETZ

notes

AWARENESS

Key concept: Do not try to re-invent the wheel
The only thing keeping you from what you want is
the awareness of how to get it!
Bob Proctor

HOW IT WORKS

If you want to have a **high** level of competency in your relationships, health, wealth and spirituality than you must be committed to continual self improvement and a life of learning. Having said that there are three primary ways to learn, "become aware". First you can read books, second through your own experiences and lastly through other peoples experiences. Awareness is the principle of education. To achieve A Total Life one must continually learn, "become aware", in all moments, everyday, in all three categories.

There are other people just like you, who were where you're at now, and got exactly where you want to go. You are not alone in your journey for *A Total Life*. There is a map, if you will, that helps us navigate to our destination and that map is in the minds of people all around us. Sometimes, our journey is finding those people who hold pieces of our map, hidden in their life experiences. Who is like us? Who has similar attributes, backgrounds, dreams, economic status, fears, and friends that has accomplished all we want to accomplish. Are you aware of people like that? Through relationships there is freedom, understanding, and hope that just as they have done "it," we can do it too. We can achieve our dreams just as they did. And, it is so much easier to accomplish your goals and implement your plan when you have a map and directions.

Like a compass, your *Design* becomes the direction, like North, and your Vision is the dial that continually points to the Design so that you can at least take steps in the right direction. You may find that to get to the places you want to go you have to let go of the

....

notes

way you thought the world was, developing Integrated solutions to get through and around the many obstacles, in the way. Finally, as you go along the road, you may find people who have traveled much of the way for you. It is so nice to just sit back and enjoy the company as you both walk toward your shared goals.

notes

Y ou have read about the importance of *Designing Your Life,* you have created a *Vision* bigger than your *Vices,* you understand the difference between chronic and acute problems, and have a hold on how important it is to take and *Integrated* approach in creating your life, and yet, you may still be wondering, "But exactly **how** do I achieve *A Total Life?* **How** do I do it?" How do I get a high level of peace and competency in relationships, health, wealth, and spirituality in all moments, holding nothing back, in any moment, over a lifetime?

This question of "how to" is a natural one, but believe it or not, the "doing" might be the simple part. It is coming into the *Awareness* of **what** to do and **how** to do it that could be the real challenge. Obviously, this book helps with *Awareness*, as the principles can guide you in the right direction and you can start implementing the suggestions now. In addition to what you have read, there are people out in the world that may hold the keys to help you better understand how to put it all together so that you can enjoy the life you dream of. As I said earlier, there are people in the world that are living the life you hope to live, not perfectly, but in a way that you can respect and appreciate. Those are the people that can help you on your journey. They can increase your *Awareness* and knowledge of how to get from concept to reality.

SHIFT PRINCIPLE

Now, for sure, you can always pick up books to help you on your journey. Books about health, wealth, relationships and spirituality will increase your competency in those areas and with more

notes
....

information you can make great strides in each area; however, books will never show you how to put it all together, *Integrate,* in such a way that the overall life is as amazing as any one of the components. Usually people go through years of trial and error trying to find that balance that gives them all they are looking for in this life. *Awareness* is the idea of finding other people, mentors or friends who have put the pieces together in a way that you admire, respect and want to emulate. Now going about finding these people is not just some random selection but below you can see that careful selection can really help.

If I wanted to be a successful business person and was looking for advice as to how I could get to a place of financial freedom, I would want to find someone who is similar to me and has accomplished what I hope to, in around the same amount of time as I wish to accomplish it. Financial freedom could mean something like developing a ball of assets or money, large enough so that a percentage of those assets give you the lifestyle you want to live. Or, it could mean going to work because you want to not because you have to. Either way, it is helpful to find someone who knows the same kinds of people you know, came from the same area, has or had the same wealth as you, and feels and thinks similar to the way you do. For example, if I use Donald Trump or Warren Buffet as models for how I should go about designing my life it would not work, for me, because Donald Trump started with his dad's money and Warren Buffett's personality is completely opposite of mine. Steve Jobs or Richard Branson more accurately fit a model that I could follow because from what I have read about those gentlemen, I have many similar traits as them.

notes

Neither of these men are accessible to me currently so they are not the best choice but a place I can start.

Having said that, below are the different types of capital that, I believe, we all have. They can serve as guides as to how to go about finding individuals who can help you on your journey. Remember, always look for those who have similar capital as you do and are where you want to be in the future.

The Four Types of Capital are as follows:

Social Capital (WHO YOU KNOW) refers to your relationships, connections, community, culture, and history.

Human Capital (HOW YOU FEEL) refers to your health, well being, attitudes, happiness, hope, and enjoyment of life.

Intellectual Capital (WHAT YOU KNOW) refers to your education, experience, and wisdom.

Financial Capital (WHAT YOU HAVE) refers to the sum of your financial assets.

There is an acronym I use to help me remember to engage with the four types of capital in such a way as to go for it **all** without making any trade-offs.

notes

SHIFT

<u>S</u>ocial + <u>H</u>uman + <u>I</u>ntellectual + <u>F</u>inancial= <u>*TOTAL LIFE*</u>

Are you *Aware* of how to marshal all four types of capital toward your *Vision*? When you become *Aware* of these four types of capital and then identify a person who has achieved success in all these areas, you will become *Aware* of how you can do the same in your life. You will have found a "wheel" that has already been invented that you can also use to carry you into *Total Life* success. Obviously, some of us do not have people in our lives right now, therefore I recommend, for those of you who do not have those people in your life, to develop a dream group. Start reading books about great leaders and people you admire. A group of three to five good biographies can really help you get clear on what is possible. In addition, at the start of this process you may need to do what I did when I was younger, and that is, just take the best parts of some of those around you while you pursue finding those who have all you desire.

What am I saying? If you want to be a millionaire in five years, find a person or persons with similar Human, Social, Intellectual, and Financial capital, as you; who has/have already accomplished your goal in the same time period you wish to; and model their behavior and actions. If you want to have an amazing marriage and be more con-nected to your children, seek out people like you that have brilliant marriages. Seek and you shall find.

When you are watching someone that is accomplished at any-thing, their competence makes it appear easy, and when they explain it, they may share some simple concepts, ideas, and strategies with you.

....

notes

But when you try them, you may find they are not necessarily easy to mimic. You will recall when we talked about chronic versus acute that there are rarely short cuts. Therefore, although you will begin to see clearly what to do, it will take consistent effort on your part. If you still think this method of finding a model and emulating will not work, ask yourself this: "Have I tried it? Have I, in all honesty, given these concepts, ideas, and strategies the time and effort needed to complete, create, and achieve a bold plan of action?"

Awareness is the idea of overvaluing, or placing more emphasis on the "how to" and undervaluing, or de-emphasizing the actual doing. *Awareness* is very similar to a childhood dream, in that the child has a great dream, but he or she may have no idea of how to get the dream to come true. This fearless childlike faith is what we all need, so that we can trust that the dream will lead and guide us in all the millions of moments that we need to make decisions to help us move toward the dream.

Those who embrace *a Total Life* do not spend their lives re-inventing the wheel. They spend the least amount of time getting the most results because they become *Aware* of how to build the house before they begin building. They have met the right people; they have researched and completed the necessary due diligence to complete the project. It was said that Walt Disney's plans to build Walt Disney World were so complete that years after he was gone, the architects and engineers needed little or no additional information to complete the project. They simply implemented the thorough, complete, detailed plans.

....

notes

When we are *Aware*, we take into consideration the best way to do something and we find the most efficient, creative, and powerful use of our resources. The idea of *Awareness* is the "how to" of living a totally successful life. What if, starting today, you lived your entire life building a computer? It is important that you start the process of creativity and development by finding the most recent, most advanced solutions first and then add and create on top of them. This would be a waste of your life because when you finally arrived at your goal, you would have created a product that has already existed for fifty plus years. Using the computer example, it would make sense to find the best computer in the world—fastest, best looking, most features, and most creative—and then begin working on how to make it better and fit your particular solution. Start at the last point of creativity in all areas, become *Aware* of what is already working and available!

By that same token, if your goal is to be spiritually connected and a great father, the only thing stopping you is the *Awareness* of how to accomplish these goals. This is when you should look around you and discover how your neighbor, pastor, priest, rabbi or mentors make it look so easy. How have they managed to reach that level of spiritual and social connectedness where you have not? It bears repeating: **The easiest way to accomplish a goal is to emulate the actions of somebody who has already achieved what you would like to achieve.** If you are *Aware* of how to do something, then the doing becomes not only do-able but, more importantly, achievable.

I am not saying lose all your creativity and just copy others. It is more like building your own dream hotel. The subcontractors are those who you use to help get the project completed. The roofing contractor, the plumbing sub contractor, and the drywall sub are all parts

notes

of your great beautiful *Design* coming to completion, but it is your *Design*, your hotel, your life, and they are just helping you get it done.

Awareness, is all about research, discovery, being curious, asking questions, learning before you act, observing, and seeing all that is happening around you as a tool for you to be able to effectively *Integrate* all the appropriate components, to fuel you *Vision*, and start to live in the *Design* you have created for yourself. Do not be the like the blind leading the blind, in that you continue to try the same things over and over again, only to constantly get the same results. That is the definition of insanity: repeating the same behavior over and over again, expecting a different result. Try a new path; get involved with the process of becoming *Aware* and you will find the secret keys that can unlock doors you have had closed for years.

The concepts in this book are broad and will work for any *Vision*. You can stand under them and allow them to create a shelter for you as an umbrella shelters you from the rain. But as you know, an umbrella only helps if you open it.

Design Your Life
Vision vs. Vice
Integration
Awareness

....

notes

I HAVE FOUND THAT IT IS MUCH EASIER
TO MAKE A SUCCESS IN LIFE THAN TO MAKE
A SUCCESS OF ONE'S LIFE.
G.W. FOLLIN

THIS LIFE IS ABOUT THIS MOMENT AND ALL THE
MOMENTS TOGETHER, WHICH WE CALL "A TOTAL LIFE."
LOUIS C. BAKER

notes

IT DOES NOT TAKE GREAT MEN TO DO THINGS, BUT IT
IS DOING THINGS THAT MAKE MEN GREAT.

ARNOLD GLASOW

THE PRICE OF GREATNESS IS RESPONSIBILITY.

WINSTON CHURCHILL

....

notes

OPEN YOUR UMBRELLA

Key concept: This book will work when you use it.

HOW TO WORK THEM

Try memorizing your goals, record them, write them down, maybe paint them on the wall and listen and live in them all the time. This will begin to change your mind, consciously and subconsciously. The mind can only focus and hold onto one thought at a time. You cannot keep these goals and this *Vision* in your mind and, at the same time, entertain all the ways you have been living that have not worked; it is a cognitive impossibility for your mind. One line of thinking must give way to another and you will notice that, at any given moment, either you are harboring the concepts presented in this book or you are operating according to the well-established, engrained thoughts with which you have always lived. An umbrella protects you from the rain, but only if you know how to open it. Make sure you are *Aware* of how to open the four key principles in this book in everyday situations, all the time.

Design Your Life
Vision vs. Vice
Integration
Awareness

These next questions will help you begin to embrace the principles of *A Total Life*. If you really want to go for this life, you might try to live in this question: "How will I imbed these principles in my mind so they will change it and help me live out the *Vision* I have *Designed* for myself?" When I say, live in the question, I mean to have the following types of **Life Audit** questions be a part of your everyday thoughts when you wake up, before bed, at lunch, and all the time.

....

notes

THE LIFE AUDIT QUESTIONS

Live in these questions:

- How will I *Design* my life for the future?
- What is my *Vision*?
- What will I do today that is congruent with the *Vision* I say I want for my future?
- Am I making trade-offs; am I settling?
- Am I working on my weakest areas?
- Am I seeking for answers as to "how I can" or settling for the answers for "why I can't?"
- What can I learn from this?

If you do not memorize and answer these questions often, it is as if you have an umbrella and do not know how to open it, thus allowing the rain of circumstances to fall on you, leaving you drenched in limitations and negativity. For a principle to work you must understand it and remember it at the appropriate time; it must become your mantra. Below are more questions to keep you thinking, *Designing*, and creating.

Examine and *Design Your Life*:

- Are you working where you want to be ten years from now?
- Are you getting healthier or sicker?
- Do you hang around with people now that you want to know twenty years from now?
- Are you where you want to be spiritually?

notes

- Will you have the money you want five years from now?
- Are you happy?
- Do you have the relationships you want?

Vision vs. Vice:
- For what would you give up everything?
- Who is most important to you and why?
- From what are your *Vices* keeping you?

Chronic versus acute—start now
- Are you expecting too much too fast?
- Are you starting today so later you can have a commendable, repeatable, respectable history?
- Are you too hard on yourself for investing years in the wrong direction?
- Are you slowly growing in the wrong direction with your
    > Marriage/ Relationships
    > Money
    > Sex
    > Business
    > Friends

Integration:
- Are you making trade-offs for no good reason?
- Are you working on your weakest areas?
- Are you relaxed?

....

notes

- What can you do that you have never done?
- Do you let the game of life play out or are you constantly fighting it?

Awareness:
- Who is someone with similar capital that is where you want to be?
- Who is going where you are going?
- Are you associating with visionaries or with naysayers?
- Who is doing what you do the best and why?
- When do the best people go for it?
- Under what model are you working?
- Is your life *Design* predictable? Based on what?

Memorize every principle and the outline of this book so you know it cold. Read each short chapter over and over again until you start *Designing* your life and creating a short-term and long-term *Vision*. Relax and understand chronic vs. acute issues. *Integrate* and stop making trade-offs, and seek *Awareness* as the answer to all of life's questions.

Below is an example of how to walk with these principles:

I have *Designed* my life to be successful in all categories.

Bottom-line: financial, legacy, budgeting, tax, investing, real estate, legal, and all business endeavors

notes

Top-Line: fun, *Vision*, values, goals, health, marriage, relationships, parenting

My *Vices* are, judging others, fear of failure, complaining, giving up too soon, fear, fear, and more fear.

My *Vision* is to inspire, motivate, and encourage others to take positive action and to live a life of total success.

Chronic versus acute: I will give myself a lifetime to realize my goals and understand that the process is as important as any short-term destination.

Integration: I will never be so irresponsible as to let my bottom-line issues kill my top-line possibilities. I will never let my bottom-line success allow me to forget why I spend time on bottom-line issues. I will not be a bicycle with no back tire or a rocket ship heading for the sun.

Awareness: For the rest of my life I am on a journey to find people who have totally successful lives. I will never be afraid to go after them and connect with them, and will, at-all-costs, submit to their wisdom and learning. If I ever come to a dead-end, I will invent a new way for those coming behind me and will share all I have learned with anyone interested in learning.

This is the great life for you, *A Total Life,* and a journey of exciting possibilities and impossible realities. It is not a destination; it is your next thought.

....

notes

JUST A REMINDER: HOW TO ENSURE THIS BOOK WILL WORK FOR YOU

The principles and concepts in this book are life transforming, but they will only transform your life if you apply them. The simplest way for this to happen is to realize that they are accessible to you at any moment. Having said that, the best way to engage with this book is to memorize the principles and then walk with them by consistently applying them to every life-scenario you experience or envision. When you have memorized the concepts, you will be amazed at how simply and easily they will help you. These concepts can be conceived of as "umbrella principles" that you can use for shelter and guidance throughout your new life journey. As you apply them, you will find yourself walking in *Total Life* success, actually living *A Total Life*— feeling great, open to possibilities, free of fear, and excited about the future.

Four simple principles:
1. *Design Your Life*
2. *Vision vs. Vice*
3. *Integration*
4. *Awareness*

....

notes

FROM THE LITTLE SPARK MAY BURST
A MIGHTY FLAME.
DANTE

ONLY HE WHO CAN SEE THE INVISIBLE
CAN DO THE IMPOSSIBLE.
FRANK L. GAINES

notes

GIVING THE 4 TIMELESS PRINCIPLES BACK

If you are anything like me and have found this book helpful in your journey and life process, and want to give the gift of A TOTAL LIFE to others, I am available for coaching, speaking, and training in the *Total Life* concepts.

For more information about the author or to purchase more books. Please send and email to inspireglobal@gmail.com

As part of my journey I educate students and children in the concepts of A Total Life in hopes to give young people a chance to design better more fulfilling lives. In addition I believe teaching financial, character, and leadership skills are keys to assisting young people on their journeys toward success. For this reason I formed, Inspire Media Group, a company focused on inspiring, motivating and encouraging people to take positive action. If you wish to donate to the cause please send an email to inspireglobal@gmail.com.

Sincerely, Louis C. Baker

....

notes

GLOSSARY OF TERMS

(Loosely defined by the author)

A Total Life: *Living a life with a high level of peace and competency in one's relationships, health, wealth, and spirituality, and holding nothing back in any moment over one's lifetime.*

Acute: *Sharp or severe in effect; intense; acute sorrow; an acute pain*

Awareness: *Informed; alert; knowledgeable; sophisticated: She is one of the most politically aware young women around.*

Balanced Life: *A life where all the main components of that life are equal in their time, competence and execution. All the components could be equally poor and that is the problem with balance.*

Capital: *Any source of profit, advantage, power, etc.*

Chronic: *Subject to a habit or pattern of behavior for a long time*

Doing Life With: *Being totally current and totally included in all the endeavors of someone's life*

Elite Net Worth: *Individuals or Families with total assets over 50 million dollars*

....

notes

Integration: *The act of bringing together or combining multiple variables into one whole or for one purpose*

Life Audit: A process of evaluating one's life by asking questions to uncover a general ranking of one's current state in connection to wealth, health, spirituality and relationships.

Possibility Exploration: *A dream building exercise whereas one creates the best possible life for him or herself*

Possibility Thinker: *A person who is in a constant state of examining what is possible, not what is predictable*

Scarcity Thinking: *A belief, thought, or way of thinking that there is a limited number of resources and we are all fighting for them*

Shift Principle: (S+H+I+F=T) *An idea that financial capital is only one component of wealth and that to achieve true wealth one needs to acquire all types of capital as seen below.*
> Social Capital *(WHO YOU KNOW)*
> *Refers to your relationships, connections, community, culture, and history.*
> Human Capital *(HOW YOU FEEL)*
> *Refers to your health, well being, attitudes, happiness, hope, and enjoyment of life.*
> Intellectual Capital *(WHAT YOU KNOW)*
> *Refers to your education, experience, and wisdom.*
> Financial Capital *(WHAT YOU HAVE)*

....

notes

Refers to the sum of your financial assets.
Total Life

The Victim: *A person who believes that other people and circumstances are the reason for their unhappiness*

Vision vs. Vice: *A concept that asserts that one is either pursuing a vision or using vice to make the day to day tolerable*

Walking With: *A way of engaging with a friend or person with whom you are spend time under a shared idea or concept: I am walking with Carol under inspire media concepts*

Worst Case Scenario Plan: *This is an exercise in which one envisions every possible event going bad for them as a way to address key fears and come to terms with potential realities before they occur.*

Holy Grail: *the idea that one event can and will change all the feelings, behaviors and circumstances in someone's life. The desire to not have to create the life you want but to have the life you want happen to you by chance. The deep longing to be rescued a hidden victim mentality.*

Stop Gap Technique: *A technique to stop negative thinking by actually yelling stop out loud or in your mind to create a break in the negative thinking.*

Scarcity: *the idea that there are not enough resources in the world for one to achieve their goals and dreams. There is a shortage of opportunity hence it is impossible to*

....

notes

achieve certain desired outcomes.   For Example: I can't build my dream there just isn't enough time.

Victim Role: *An attitude that other people, circumstances or events are the reason you are unhappy, unsuccessful or not accomplishing your goals and dreams*

Vision: *the fuel of life, the energy, the want to, the visualization, the hope, the passion, the guiding light, the truth, the opposite of apathetic*

Umbrella Principle: *a principle or idea that when fully understood can help an individual through tough and challenging times*

. . . .

notes

4831036R00066

Made in the USA
San Bernardino, CA
09 October 2013